CONGREGATION FOR THE DOCTRINE
OF THE FAITH

TO PROMOTE
AND SAFEGUARD
THE FAITH

*From the Holy Office
to the Congregation for the Doctrine of the Faith*

LIBRERIA EDITRICE VATICANA

ISBN 978-88-209-9624-6

www.vatican.va

www.libreriaeditricevaticana.va

PREFACE

The Pastors of the Church, who have the mission to proclaim the word of salvation received by divine Revelation, are required to safeguard in its entirety the deposit of faith entrusted to them by Christ. Throughout the many centuries of the Church's history, the Popes have been assisted by various entities to help them better fulfill this responsibility, according to the needs of each age. Over time different offices have facilitated the governance of the Church by assuring observance of laws that have been promulgated, encouraging initiatives to accomplish the goals proper to the Church, and resolving controversies which arise. The origin of the Congregation for the Doctrine of the Faith is situated in this context. Recent documentary research on the history of this institution has produced a picture of the Congregation less darkly drawn than was formerly the case, a picture which can help overcome ideological prejudices and dispel commonly-held misconceptions. This new image is also aided by significant editorial efforts that have made available to the wider public documents previously known only by a limited number of scholars.

Progress in these studies has been encouraged by the opening of the historical archives of the Congregation for the Doctrine of the Faith. On that occasion, the then Prefect, Cardinal Joseph Ratzinger, remarked: "The opening of our Archives is inspired by the same charge given to our Congregation by the Holy Father to 'promote and safeguard the doctrine of the faith and morals for the whole Catholic world'. I am certain that opening our Archives responds not only to legitimate desires of scholars, but also to the Church's determined intention to serve man by helping him to understand himself by reading his own history without prejudice. (Card. Joseph Ratzinger, "The Dream of Truth", *Avvenire.* 23 Jan 1998, p. 210)".

This little work sees the light of day in this new, positive context. Its purpose is both informational (historical presentation) and formational (education in the faith). The following topics are treated here: the origin and development of the Holy Office; its reform at the beginning of the twentieth century; the Congregation for the Doctrine of the Faith; and the Dicastery according to the Apostolic Constitution *Pastor bonus*. There is also detailed information concerning: the structure and organization of the Congregation for the Doctrine of the Faith, (personnel, offices and procedures); its examination of doctrine and the norms for reserved delicts; and the other offices associated with it: the Pontifical

Biblical Commission, the International Theological Commission, and the Pontifical Commission *Ecclesia Dei*.

Like other offices of the Roman Curia, the Congregation for the Doctrine of the Faith is an institution of ecclesiastical right, assisting the Holy Father in his universal mission as regards doctrine of faith and morals. It has the responsibility to watch over the profession of the true faith and guide all activities of the Church related to that faith: liturgy, preaching, catechesis, the spiritual life, ecumenical endeavors, social teaching, etc.

In the context in which society and the Church exist today – a context marked by rapid cultural, political, technical, and economic change, and by public opinion increasingly shaped by patterns and directions influenced by the social media – the Congregation for the Doctrine of the Faith is confronted on a daily basis with a difficult challenge.

The Congregation strives to discern the key thoughts and most important ideas that emerge from the ebb and flow of cultural challenges and theological opinions. It is necessary, therefore, to examine these challenges, explore them to their deepest roots, and evaluate them in a way that is inspired by the Gospel and Catholic tradition. This work is carried out in conformity to the specific nature of the Church as the People of God in its two dimensions as a universal and a local community.

The Congregation's life is full of colloquiums, study sessions, and a great deal of correspondence with bishops, nuncios, and superiors of institutes throughout the world. Its cooperation with other offices of the Holy See becomes more intense when they are developing official documents and reaching decisions that involve the doctrine of the faith and the moral life. This helps to explain the association of the Pontifical Biblical Commission and the International Theological Commission with the Congregation, both of which provide consultative assistance in various fields according to the expertise of their members. At the same time, the documents they produce advance a deepening understanding of the faith for the whole Church.

The Congregation listens, too – in a particular way during the periodic visits of bishops *ad limina*: on these occasions, all the bishops have an opportunity to share the particular problems they face in their own countries and to seek advice. Occasionally, some representatives of the Congregation will travel to different continents to meet with the presidents of the doctrinal commissions of Episcopal Conferences to examine relevant doctrinal problems with them. The Congregation also studies theological journals from throughout the world in order to be continually informed of new developments in theology. In the case of extremely difficult questions, the Congregation itself provides an opportunity for a more profound understanding by holding symposia involving experts from throughout the world.

It is my hope that this work will provide a helpful tool for the faithful to grow and mature in the faith, so that the word of God will continually spread and bear fruit.

GERHARD Card. MÜLLER
Prefect

Vatican City, 30th April 2015
Memorial of St. Pius V,
Patron of the Congregation

TO PROMOTE AND SAFEGUARD THE FAITH

*From the Holy Office to the Congregation
of the Doctrine of the Faith*

The whole Church has been entrusted with handing on the Christian faith. Every Christian shares in this fundamental duty, but the Pope and the bishops in communion with the Church of Rome have a particular responsibility to promote and safeguard the faith. From the earliest centuries there has been a concern to defend orthodox belief in Christianity, although the way to accomplish this has differed and undergone development in various historical contexts.

The medieval Inquisition came into existence in the first half of the thirteenth century, during the pontificate of Gregory IX (1227-1241), its purpose being to suppress heresy in all its forms. At the beginning of this epoch the suppression of heresy, which had formerly been the responsibility of diocesan bishops, came to be exercised also by the Holy See directly, and special legates were appointed for this purpose. Later, this work was undertaken by religious orders, in particular the Dominicans and Franciscans. From this developed a characteristic ecclesiastical institution – the Inquisition – which consisted of a network of tribunals, whose leaders were given express pontifical delegation to judge and, if need be, condemn those charged with the crime of heresy. Following a practice in force in all European judicial systems until the end of the eighteenth century, this process made allowance for the use of torture in certain very specific circumstances, and, in the most serious cases, for condemnation to death by burning. Civil authority (the so-called "secular arm") carried out the death sentence. In fact, the temporal powers were generally eager to assist in the struggle against heresy, because the heretic was perceived to be a threat to society at large.

ORIGIN AND DEVELOPMENT OF THE HOLY OFFICE

By the middle of the fifteenth century, the institution of the Inquisition entered into a period of decline. With the extinction of mass movements of heresy (such as the Cathars), some tribunals were disbanded, while others became inactive or saw their judicial activity greatly reduced.

A new phase in the history of the Inquisition opened with the establishment of the Spanish Inquisition. In 1478 Sixtus IV, in response to a forceful request by the Catholic rulers, Isabella of Castille and Ferdinand of Aragon, agreed to restore and extend the Inquisition to the kingdoms and dominions of the Iberian Peninsula. The concession was prompted by an alarm created by the spread of Crypto-Judaism, a heresy embraced by Jewish converts to Christianity who, after having received baptism, returned in a clandestine way to the practice of their ancestors' religion.

Following an initial period of transition, the system established itself according to the following pattern: the sovereigns submitted to the Pope the name of a candidate to be Inquisitor General of Spain (the "royal right of presentation"). The Pope would confer upon him jurisdiction in matters concerning offenses against the faith and grant the faculty for him to sub-delegate his proper authority to regional inquisitors. Local tribunals enforced Pontifical inquisitorial law, although subsequent privileges had the effect of granting to the internal workings of these tribunals a certain amount of autonomy in respect to papal authority.

During these same years, the so-called Roman Inquisition was established. Arising from the ashes of the medieval Inquisition, it was instituted to combat and suppress the spread of the doctrines of the Reformers into the Italian peninsula. In the face of the growth of Protestantism, Paul III had in fact instituted, with the Constitution *Licet ab initio* of 12 July, 1542, a special commission of six cardinals who were competent to judge offenses in matters of faith. It is very likely that from the outset these cardinals were assisted by theologians and canonists in the capacity of consultors. In the years immediately following, the organizational structure of the

Commission grew: at some time, certainly not later than 1548, the Master of the Sacred Palace (the former name for the Theologian of the Pontifical Household) became a member *ex officio*; in 1551, the position of Commissioner was created, who served as Secretary; and in 1553 this last was joined by a prelate with the title of Assessor.

This organization – then called the Congregation of the Holy Roman and Universal Inquisition (or Congregation of the Holy Office), whose sphere of influence, at least in theory, should extend to the entire Christian world, starting from Italy and the Roman Curia – had the faculty to send its own delegates, where necessity demanded, who could judge possible appeals and had the power to act against apostates, heretics, those suspected of heresy and their defenders, followers, and supporters, regardless of their office or dignity. The general inquisitors could also have recourse to the secular arm.

To establish the universal character of the Roman Inquisition, which was explicitly stated in its name, would mean to centralize jurisdiction in the matter of heresy in Rome, the seat of the Papacy. In fact, as will be seen elsewhere, such universal jurisdiction was not fully exercised prior to the beginning of the nineteenth century.

One of the first official acts of Julius III was to confirm the Roman and Universal Inquisition at the beginning of 1550. The Pope determined that it would concern itself primarily with religious life in Italy, where he had been warned that there were still many heretics. He also confirmed that it was the central authority responsible for proceeding judicially in defense of the faith in all Christian countries. The Pope published on 15 February 1551 the Constitution *Licet a diversis*, which condemned the claim of the civil authorities of some states that they were authorized to interfere in the process of charging heretics, as had been attempted, for example, in the Republic of Venice.

Cardinal Gian Pietro Carafa, who was an ardent supporter of the Roman Inquisition from its inception and had shown himself to be one of the most active of the general inquisitors, ascended to the papal throne in May, 1555, taking the name Paul IV. He immediately devoted himself to developing this institution, and for this purpose he repaired its offices on the Via di Ripetta, which he himself had purchased as a cardinal at his own expense when the Inquisition was established in 1542. With the motu proprio of 11 February 1556, *Attendentes onera*, the Pope extended a series of privileges and fiscal exemptions to the building and those who served there; further, he granted new faculties to the members of the tribunal, greatly expanding their sphere of jurisdiction. This went far beyond the confines of dogma, strictly speaking, and authorized them to investigate the crimes of pandering, rape, prostitution, and sodomy; later, they were charged to investigate allegations of "heretical simony" according to the definition of Paul IV himself, which included selling the sacraments, conferring ordination on underage candidates, abuses regarding benefices, and the like. In view of the wider responsibilities of this tribunal, the Pope increased the number of Cardinal members: between December 1558 and May 1559, seventeen Cardinals were added to the Congregation.

On the very day of Paul IV's death (18 August 1559) an angry mob, reacting to the stringent methods of the inquisitors, sacked the seat of the Tribunal on the Via di Ripetta, scattering and destroying the records of its procedural acts. Paul IV's successor, Pius IV, was shocked by this and immediately set about reducing the excessive power accorded to the Inquisition and its members by Paul IV. Abandoning his initial idea of abolishing the Inquisition altogether, Pius IV sought to return its ordinary functions to a reasonable level. He began, in a congregation of 11 January 1560, by reducing the jurisdictional authority of the Cardinal inquisitors, restoring the proper competence of the institution to matters concerning the protection of the integrity of the faith.

Recognizing the effectiveness of the activity undertaken by the Holy Office up to that time, with the Constitution *Pastoralis officii munus* of 14 October 1562, Pius IV newly delineated the activities of the Cardinal members, determining at the same time the exact limits of their jurisdiction, which became broader. On October 31st, with the motu proprio *Saepius inter arcana*, he confirmed that the Roman Inquisition had the power to carry out processes against prelates, bishops, archbishops, patriarchs, and cardinals, always reserving to the Pope, however, the right to pronounce final sentence in consistory. Again, with the motu proprio *Cum sicut accepimus* of 2 August 1564, he reduced to eight the number of cardinal inquisitors (formerly there had been a total of twenty-three), adding a ninth, however, to clarify their functions. Finally, with the motu proprio *Cum inter crimina* of the following August 27th, he granted cardinal inquisitors the faculty to possess and read heretical literature and other prohibited books, and to permit others in turn to possess and read such works.

The Dominican Michele (in the world, Antonio) Ghislieri, who had served as Commissioner of the Inquisition since its founding and had been cardinal inquisitor under Paul IV, became Pope on 17 January 1566, taking the name Pius V. He furnished the organization with new offices. This had been rendered necessary by the destruction of the original site on the via di Ripetta, after which the cardinal inquisitors had been required to meet in the home of their senior member. To that end, Pius V acquired and set about restoring a building located near the site where the Vatican basilica was undergoing construction. Work on the basilica was interrupted for the purpose of hastening the reconstruction of the new palace of the Holy Office. This building was useable as early as 1569, but was only completed in 1586, when Sixtus V attached a prison to it. This was torn down in the last century (1921-1925) during work to enlarge the palace which is now occupied for the most part by the offices of the Congregation for the Doctrine of the Faith.

Pius V also ordered the establishment of an appropriate archive in which to preserve all the procedural acts. It was strictly forbidden to make copies of these, although they could be consulted on the spot in case of need; confidentiality was strictly enforced regarding all matters concerning questions in the processes, and a violation of this was viewed as a personal insult to the Pope. Later, arrangements were made to protect the Cardinal inquisitors and their assistants from threats or violence, and to safeguard witnesses from harassment or reprisals from the accused themselves or from their relatives and friends. With the motu proprio *Cum felicis recordationis* of 5 December 1571, the Pope decreed that the involvement of only two cardinals was sufficient for decisions of the Holy Office to be valid, rather than three, as was prescribed for every other curial office.

The Congregation of the Index was attached to the Sacred Roman and Universal Inquisition; it had been begun by Pius V in 1571, but was only formally established by his successor, Gregory XIII, on 13 September 1573. Its specific purpose was to examine suspect works, to correct or edit those books which, after the required review by censors, were allowed to continue to circulate, and to add periodically to the list of forbidden books (*Index librorum prohibitorum*).

Within fifty years of its establishment the Holy Roman Office attained an absolutely privileged position in the process of a general reorganization of the central government of the Church and the Papal States brought about by Sixtus V with the Constitution *Immensa aeterni Dei* of 22 January 1588. In fact, at the head of the fifteen congregations established by Sixtus V (which included the five already existing congregations) was placed the *Congregatio sanctae Inquisitionis haereticae pravitatis*, which preserved its character as a tribunal.

Placed under the direct supervision of the Pope because of the important matters it dealt with, the Roman Inquisition came to be endowed with greater powers by Sixtus V; the result was that anything concerning the faith came within its jurisdictional responsibility. Its power extended not only to Rome and the Papal States, but to every place and person: Latin and Eastern Catholics alike were answerable to it. The only exceptions were the Spanish and Portuguese Inquisitions, whose respective privileges could only be modified with the explicit agreement of the Pope. However, although the Congregation enjoyed universal jurisdiction in theory, a study of the documents of the time shows that, apart from Italian tribunals, the Roman Inquisition exercised its authority only in Malta, Avignon (at that time a Pontifical dominion), Besançon, Carcassone, Toulouse (in France), and Cologne (the Holy Roman Empire of Germany).

In any case, the Congregation held absolute jurisdiction in all matters pertaining to offenses concerning the faith – heresy, schism, apostasy, divination, witchcraft, magic – and had the faculty to dispense from the impediments of mixed religion and disparity of cult, with special competence regarding the so-called Pauline Privilege for dissolving a matrimonial bond. The Congregation also was responsible for all matters which, although not directly concerning the faith, were related to it: the crime of solicitation *ad turpia*, religious vows, the observance of feast days, and fasting and abstinence.

Although the Sistine constitution said nothing about it, the Congregation was also responsible for the censure and proscription of books recognized to be heretical, once the suspect books had been examined by the Congregation of the Index and its decision was confirmed by Sixtus V. The Congregation of the Index integrated its activity with the work of the section of the Inquisition dedicated to writings; responsible as it was for the most serious questions regarding faith and morals, it was proving impossible for the Inquisition to exercise complete supervision over printed works, which were being published in great numbers everywhere.

The great importance accorded to the Congregation of the Inquisition by Sixtus V increased the desire of cardinals to belong to it. Following the complete reorganization of the Roman Curia by Sixtus, the Congregation of the Inquisition maintained its pre-eminent place among the various congregations. It remained almost entirely unchanged in its structure and its institutional responsibilities up to the beginning of the nineteenth century.

With the Constitution *Universi dominici gregis* of 30 August 1622 Gregory XV confirmed the competence of the Congregation of the Inquisition to deal with the crime of solicitation *ad turpia*, a competence reaffirmed by Benedict XIV with the Constitution *Sollicita ac provida* of 9 July 1753, which he developed and wrote personally. The Pope exhorted the members of the Congregation of the Index to undertake a more attentive and impartial examination of works submitted to prevent complaints by their authors. He arranged to have the theologians joined by men renowned for their culture, to have more objective processes, and to hear from the accused or their representatives. The Pope tried to settle the question, never resolved, of the overlapping jurisdictions of the Holy Office and the Congregation of the Index concerning censorship. He determined that the latter should concern itself solely with works expressly condemned as dangerous, but only if they had not already undergone an examination by the Congregation of the Index.

Toward the end of the eighteenth century the Congregation of the Inquisition was entrusted with some offenses that were not concerned, strictly speaking, with doctrinal matters. During the pontificate of Pius VI it was also given responsibility for everything having to do with Holy Orders, both dogmatic and disciplinary matters.

In the nineteenth century, Gregory XVI also entrusted the Inquisition with the causes of saints for a time, in matters touching on doctrine and in determining what constitutes martyrdom.

THE REORGANIZATION AT THE BEGINNING OF THE TWENTIETH CENTURY

One final extension of the responsibilities of the Congregation of the Inquisition, prior to a major reform of the Curia carried out by Pius X in 1908, was brought about by this same Pope with the motu proprio *Romanis pontificibus* of 17 December 1903, in virtue of which it was decreed that the former Congregation for the Election of Bishops be merged with the Holy Office. With some appropriate exceptions, all material pertaining to the selection and promotion of bishops was to be submitted to the Holy Office, except for those that were the responsibility of the Congregation for the Propagation of the Faith and the Congregation for Extraordinary Ecclesiastical Affairs, respectively.

More varied and important changes were made to the old Congregation of the Holy Roman and Universal Inquisition by the first total reorganization of the Roman Curia in the twentieth century. This was almost entirely a personal initiative of Pius X, and it passed through five different plans – one of which was formulated by the Pope himself – and was completed by him with the Constitution *Sapienti consilio* of 29 June 1908. The purpose of the reorganization was to impart a modern direction to the various curial structures so that they could respond to the changing demands of the times.

With regard to various areas of responsibility, everything pertaining to the observance of the precepts of the Church devolved to the Congregation of the Council (today the Congregation for the Clergy), which was welcomed by the same Pius X in his personal project of reform. Matters pertaining to the selection of bishops was transferred to the Congregation of the Consistory (now the Congregation for Bishops), and the dispensation from religious vows was reserved to the new Congregation of Religious (today the Congregation for Consecrated Life and Societies of Apostolic Life). Matters concerning Indulgences were now to be referred to the Holy Office.

In the wake of the Constitution *Sapienti consilio* the *Ordo servandus in Sacris Congregationibus, Tribunalis, Officiis Romanae Curiae* was published, which contained general and particular norms to be observed by each congregation and the various offices of the Roman Curia. It was formally established that the highest positions in the Holy Office would be the Assessor and the Commissary. The Holy Office was directed to draft as soon as possible its *ratio agendi*, and this was published in 1911 with the name *Lex et ordo Sancti Officii*; it established the norms proper to the Congregation, indicating precisely the roles, functions, and structures of the Holy Office.

Following the reorganization of Pius X, the renewed Congregation of the Holy Office maintained its first place among the various Roman congregations, and subsequently had the word "Supreme" added to its title because its President was the Pope himself. Its jurisdictional competence remained the defense of the doctrine of the faith and morals, processes against heresy, as well as other offenses that created a suspicion of heresy (the celebration of Mass or hearing of confessions by one who was not ordained a priest, solicitation *ad turpia* by a priest in confession, divination, witchcraft, casting spells, etc.), the granting of the Pauline Privilege and dispensations from the impediments of disparity of cult and mixed religion, and all matters pertaining to Indulgences.

Benedict XV addressed the specific responsibilities of the Holy Office, decreeing in his motu proprio *Alloquentes* of 25 March 1917 the suppression of the Congregation of the Index as an autonomous office and its reintegration into the Holy Office. This had originally been considered at the time of the reorganization of Pius X and was rendered necessary to avoid conflicts regarding the competence of each of the two congregations. In order to lessen the burdens placed on the Holy Office, in this same document Benedict XV removed responsibility for all matters touching on Indulgences (with the exception of a doctrinal review of new prayers and devotions) and entrusted this to the Apostolic Penitentiary.

Following the reorganization brought about by Pius X, the presidency of the Holy Office continued to be reserved to the Pope, who ordinarily exercised his activity through the Cardinal Secretary, a position traditionally held by the Dean of the Cardinal members of the Congregation, who were called General Inquisitors (the last time this title was used was in a decree of 2 August 1929). The structure of the Congregation of the Holy Office comprised a certain number of officials. The first two, called "greater", were the Assessor and the Commissary. The Assessor, from the secular clergy, assisted the Cardinal Secretary to deal with ordinary matters and general discipline. The Commissary, a Dominican, had the responsibility to provide for judicial inquiries in penal cases that must adjudicated by the Congregation in its function as a tribunal, he was assisted by a "first associate" and a "second associate", also Dominicans. All three of these Dominicans came from the Lombardy province of the Order of Preachers in virtue of a privilege accorded to that province by Pius V, who, when he served as Commissary from 1551 to 1556, had been a religious of that province. The third major official of the Congregation was the *Sostituto*, responsible for the special section of the Congregation dealing with Indulgences, during the ten years that this was within the competence of the Congregation (1908-1917).

The minor officials of the Congregation consisted of: two advocates, one of whom was called "fiscale" (until 1920, and from then on known as the Promotor of Justice) and the other "of the accused", who had the responsibility both to present the charge and to act as defense counsel for those accused who are either unable or unwilling to choose their own defender; a *sommista*, who prepared a summary of the process; a notary, with some assistants, for the drafting of the acts of the process; and an archivist, responsible for organizing and safeguarding documents.

Numerous consultors also served the Congregation, chosen from among secular and religious clergy, theologians and jurists. Following an ancient right, among these were the Master General of the Dominicans, the Master of the Sacred Palace, and a theologian who was a member of the Conventual Franciscans; these were known as *consultori nati* ("natural consultors") of the Holy Office. In addition to these, there were joined to the Congregation various *qualificatori* ("qualifiers") who were a particular category of advisers (not to be confused with consultors) chosen from among the most eminent theologians and canonists residing in Rome. They were called upon to submit in writing, subject to examination by the consultors, the degree of error found in a book or teaching submitted to the Congregation for judgment. The norms pertaining to the restructuring of the Congregation of the Holy Office that emerged from the reorganization undertaken by Pius X and the modifications made by Benedict XV were included in canon 247 of the *Codex iuris canonici* published in 1917.

THE CONGREGATION FOR THE DOCTRINE OF THE FAITH

The greatly altered cultural, social and political circumstances of the contemporary world led the fathers of the Second Vatican Council to seek an updating of the offices of the Roman Curia; this was expressed especially in the Decree *Christus Dominus* of 28 October 1965, which called for a general reorganization of the entire curial structure. The reform of the Curia had been one of the earliest proposals set forth by Paul VI, which he himself stated in his famous discourse to the members of the Curia on 21 September 1963. Among other things, he said: "Many years have passed; thus, it is understandable that venerable age itself would have a deleterious effect on its organization, so that a disparity is felt between its structure and procedures and the demands and practices of the contemporary world. There is a need both to simplify and decentralize and, at the same time, to expand [the Curia] and equip it for new functions". While a special commission of Cardinals worked on this project, Paul VI himself anticipated the reorganization of the most prestigious and debated office of the Roman Curia, the Supreme Sacred Congregation of the Holy Office, and issued the motu proprio *Integrae servandae* on 7 December 1965, on the very eve of the Council's conclusion. This motu proprio is reproduced in the Appendix of this document.

The recognition of the right to a defense of any "accused" author was one of the most important innovations introduced by the motu proprio *Integrae servandae*. This document aimed at addressing one of the major criticisms made about the Holy Office: the impossibility for an author to defend his work when it was being examined by the Congregation with the intent of putting it on the Index; some presumed that the Index had been abolished because it was never mentioned in the motu proprio of Paul VI.

Confronted with interpretations of this sort on the part of many bishops, Cardinal Alfredo Ottaviani, Pro-Prefect of the Congregation for the Doctrine of the Faith, published a special Notification on 14 June 1966 describing the arrangements for safeguarding faith and morals in published works. He stated that, although the Index no longer had the weight of ecclesiastical law with sanctions, its moral value continued in full force because it reminded the Christian conscience that, on the basis of natural law, books that are harmful to faith and morals should not be read. The same Congregation then published *Nuntius*, a special bulletin to underscore this idea, and to help priests and the faithful to evaluate and avoid such books; this appeared in early 1967, but was not subsequently published again. Then, in a decree of 15 November 1966 the Congregation for the Doctrine of the Faith specified that it intended to abrogate canon 1599 (the list of prohibited books) and canon 2318 (the excommunication of authors, publishers, readers and possessors of this particular category of books) of the *Codex iuris canonici* of 1917.

The original name Holy Roman and Universal Inquisition had already been abandoned in 1908, because it was so associated with the memory of the excessive, despised rigor of former times. The new name, the Sacred Congregation for the Doctrine of the Faith, was adopted in 1965 as being more descriptive of the actual work of the Congregation, and replaced the name Sacred Congregation of the Holy Office, which had always distinguished this entity for the first four centuries of its existence. At the same time, the qualification Supreme was also dropped, which had declared the supremacy of this Congregation over other curial offices, although in recent times such supremacy had only been honorific.

Along with the name, the functions proper to this Congregation underwent a radical transformation: rather than prosecuting heresies and suppressing offenses against the faith, its purpose was to promote and safeguard the faith. The granting of dispensations for mixed religion and disparity of cult were removed from the jurisdictional sphere of the Congregation. Further modifications were made to the composition of the Congregation: the Commissary and two assistants disappeared, as well as the entire category of "Qualifiers".

The normative ratification of the motu proprio of 1965 was accomplished completely in the general reform of the Roman Curia brought about by Paul VI in the Constitution *Regimini Ecclesiae universae* of 15 August 1967. Certain other changes had been made in the interval between the motu proprio and the Constitution. The most noteworthy were a decision relative to the leadership of the Congregation – no longer reserved to the Pope, but entrusted, with all its inherent powers, to a Cardinal, as in all the other Roman Congregations – and the inclusion in the highest levels of the Congregation of some diocesan bishops as full members, in conformity with the motu proprio *Pro comperto sane* of 6 August 1967. The primary responsibility of the Congregation of the Doctrine of the Faith continued to be to promote and safeguard doctrine regarding faith and morals throughout the Catholic world.

THE CONGREGATION ACCORDING TO THE CONSTITUTION *PASTOR BONUS*

This direction was confirmed by the Constitution *Pastor bonus* of 28 June 1988, with which

John Paul II reorganized the Roman Curia. He entrusted to it the responsibility to encourage "studies aimed at increasing the understanding of the faith" and to see to it that "it is possible to respond in the light of faith to new problems that emerge from the progress of science and civilization" (Article 49). The Congregation for the Doctrine of the Faith's work is no longer limited exclusively to the defense of the faith; its principal task is to promote doctrine. The Congregation should assist bishops, both individually and in episcopal groups, in their primary role as authoritative teachers and doctors of the faith, whose integrity they themselves were to bear witness, and of which they should be vigilant custodians and ardent promoters (Article 50).

In order to act on behalf of faith and morals, the Congregation for the Doctrine of the Faith exercises its mandate by seeking to obviate harm that can come from errors that have been disseminated in any way. To this end, it seeks to insure that writings concerning faith and morals be subject to prior examination by the competent authority. It examines writings and opinions that seem contrary or dangerous to right faith, and if it is determined that they are contrary to the teaching of the Church – the respective authors, however, having been provided an opportunity to explain thoroughly their ideas – then they will be reproved in due time, having forewarned the Ordinary concerned, and suitable remedies will be brought to bear, if this be opportune. Finally, the

Congregation sees to it that errors or dangerous doctrines which have spread among the Christian people do not lack an adequate rebuttal (Article 51).

In conformity with Article 52, it falls again within the competence of the Congregation for the Doctrine of the Faith to judge delicts against the faith and more grave delicts against morals or in the celebration of the sacraments that are reported to it and, if necessary, to proceed to declare or to inflict canonical sanctions according to the norm of law, either common or proper (law).

Having responsibility for what concerns the privilege of the faith, according to Article 53 of *Pastor bonus*, the Congregation has the duty to examine the reasons for the dissolution of a marital bond between a baptized and unbaptized party or between two unbaptized parties when the Pauline Privilege is not applied.

To foster the uniformity of doctrinal teaching in the life of the Church, the Constitution *Pastor bonus* (Article 54) directs that documents published by other offices of the Roman Curia, insofar as they touch on the doctrine of faith or morals, are subject to the prior judgment of the Congregation. This authority to examine is explicitly mentioned and confirmed other places in the Constitution: in Article 73, where it states that the Congregation for the Causes of Saints should request the *votum* of the Congregation for the Doctrine of the Faith regarding the eminent doctrine of a saint who has been nominated to be a Doctor of the Church; in Article 94, which directs that the Congregation for the Clergy should seek the approval of the Congregation for the publication of catechisms and other writings intended for catechetical instruction; in Article 137, where it says that the Pontifical Council for the Promotion of Christian Unity should work in close cooperation with the Congregation for the Doctrine of the Faith, especially when it intends to produce public documents or declarations, since the Council often deals with matters which by their very nature touch on the doctrine of the faith; and, finally, in Article 161, where the Pontifical Council for Inter-religious Dialogue must work in consultation with the Dicastery where the matter so requires.

Following the changes introduced in 1965 and confirmed in subsequent legislation, the Congregation no longer has any jurisdiction concerning the discipline of mixed marriages and related matters, which, in accordance with canons 1124-1129, is now dealt with by the local Ordinary, except for cases involving the dissolution of marriages in favor of the faith. Nor is the Eucharistic fast for celebrating priests within its competence.

In the exercise of its institutional functions, without limits of territory or persons (except Cardinals), in addition to its ordinary administrative power and ordinary power to dispense graces (for example, the lifting of censures or irregularities) the Congregation also possesses a strictly jurisdictional power because it functions both as a forum of grace and as a tribunal in the proper sense, proceeding as a court of first instance or court of appeals against the offenses of heresy, schism, apostasy of the faith, as well as the more grave delicts (*delicta graviora*) against morals or in the celebration of the sacraments.

Personnel, Offices, Procedures

Prior to the major reform of the Roman Curia in the late sixteenth century, the older Congregation of the Holy Office was presided over by a Cardinal with the title of Head, and later Prefect. However, in light of the sensitive matters dealt with by this Congregation, in 1588 Sixtus V chose to reserve the leadership to the Pope. Popes held this position for nearly four centuries, represented however in day the day to day workings of the Congregation by a Cardinal Secretary. This remained the state of affairs until Paul VI changed the title to Pro-Prefect. The following official notice appeared in the *Osservatore Romano* on 9 February 1966: "By the order of His Holiness to the most eminent lord Cardinals who direct the Sacred Congregation of the Doctrine of the Faith, the Consistorial Congregation, and the Congregation for the Oriental Church, of which the Holy Father is Prefect; they will now be known as Pro-Prefects, and the Assessors and *Sostituti* will be respectively Secretary and Undersecretary." The title changed again on 1 March 1968 when the Constitution *Regimini Ecclesiae universae* (n. 42) went into effect, which determined that the Cardinals of each of the Congregations would have the title Prefect. In this way the Congregation for the Doctrine of the Faith came into line with normal practice of the Roman Curia. Also, the word "sacred" was dropped from the title, as with other congregations, after the publication of the Constitution *Pastor bonus* of John Paul II in 1988.

Along with the Cardinal Prefect, who today directs the Congregation, there are other Cardinals, some diocesan bishops, the Secretary, the Undersecretary, the Promotor of Justice, and an adequate number of officials of various levels (*capi ufficio, aiutanti di studio, addetti di segretaria, addetti tecnici e scrittori*) distributed among the various offices that make up the Congregation. The Congregation is assisted as well by thirty consultors appointed by the Pope who are recognized throughout the Catholic world for their doctrine, prudence, and expertise, and who can represent the particular perspectives of various cultures. Should the matter under discussion require it, experts can be added drawn from those teaching various disciplines in the Roman universities, who can also be invited to take part, if necessary, at the meetings of the *Consulta*.

The Secretary – known until 1966 as the Assessor – is the Prefect's closest collaborator. He assists with the overall operation of the Congregation, prepares material to be submitted to the Ordinary and Plenary Sessions, assigns consultors to examine the most important and delicate questions and presides at their meetings, distributes the work among the various officials and follows their activity. He is assisted in these various functions by the Undersecretary (a recent position), who can also stand in for the Secretary when he is away or cannot be present.

To the Promotor of Justice (until 1920 known as the Fiscal Advocate), whose presence indicates the role of the Congregation as a tribunal, falls the responsibility to deal in judicial way with delicts against the faith and the more grave delicts in the celebration of the sacraments. He carefully oversees the correct application of canon and proper law in the carrying out of penal processes and the application of penalties. It is his responsibility to initiate, lead and guide the processes, look after the questioning of the one being investigated and the witnesses, compile rebuttals to the arguments made by the advocates for the accused, propose the punishment to be imposed. He is the first person to examine possible appeals or recourses and refer them to the appropriate office.

The doctrinal office is concerned with matters having to do with the promotion and safeguarding of doctrine in regards to faith and morals. It prepares documents intended to promote the Church's teaching and issue clarifications when confronted with views that differ from the teaching of the Magisterium, as well as the examination of writings and other opinions that appear to be dangerous because they are contrary to right faith. This office also reviews the doctrinal aspect of documents produced by other congregations. It also considers, from a doctrinal point of view, requests to determine that there is no obstacle to making an appointment or granting an honor.

The disciplinary office deals with delicts against the faith and the more grave delicts against morals and in the celebration of the sacraments. It is also responsible for examining other problems connected with the discipline of the faith, such as cases of false mysticism, claims of apparitions, spiritualism, magic, and simony. It deals with admission to the priesthood of men who were formerly ministers in non-Catholic religions; dispensations from irregularities or impediments to the reception of Holy Orders that fall within the competency of the Congregation; and absolution for excommunications reserved to the Holy See, except when these are dealt with by the Apostolic Penitentiary. It also considers, from a disciplinary point of view, requests to determine that there is no obstacle to making an appointment or granting an honor.

The matrimonial office deals with what concerns the *privilegium fidei*. It investigates reasons for the dissolution of marriages *in favorem fidei*, and, consequently, with doubts concerning the validity of baptism, and, in cooperation with the doctrinal office, other aspects of the matrimonial bond.

Depending on the nature of the questions to be discussed or matters to be handled, the Congregation acts with lesser or greater solemnity through, respectively, *Congressi*, *Consulte*, ordinary sessions, and plenary sessions.

The following take part in meetings of the *Congresso*: the Prefect, the Secretary, the Undersecretary, the Promotor of Justice (for questions coming within his competence), the head of the office responsible for the matter under discussion, as well as other officials following the case; another official records the decisions. The *Congresso* deliberates about the granting of licenses, dispensations, and absolutions; it decides questions of subordinate offices; it indicates the procedure for the examination of writings, following the norms of the *Agendi ratio*; it appoints experts who will make up the commission to study a matter and the person who will act as relator on behalf of the author; it determines the questions to be directed to the *Consulta*, the ordinary session, and to special commissions; it proposes to the ordinary session the convocation of symposia or scientific meetings to encourage the examination of issues that will foster a growth in understanding of the faith.

The *Consulta* is convened and presided over by the Secretary of the Congregation; the consultors appointed by the Congregation, or at least some of them; the Undersecretary and Promotor of Justice in questions pertaining to their competence, and an official responsible for recording the minutes. The members of the *Consulta* examine in a collegial manner the questions submitted to them – accompanied by the necessary documentation and the report from the office – and record in writing the reasons for their opinion. The *Consulta* can be either general or restricted, except in interdisciplinary matters when consultors are drawn from diverse theological schools; other persons with particular expertise can be added, without the right to vote. When the unusual nature of a matter demands special study, the Congregation can ask for the private opinion of persons with special expertise, who will ordinarily submit their opinion in writing; and it can also establish a special commission to study a matter, made up of experts designated by the *Congresso*.

The ordinary session ordinarily meets on Wednesday, attended by at least five members resident in Rome, possibly other voting members (which includes the Secretary), the Undersecretary, who does not vote but records the minutes, and the Promotor of Justice when there are matters that come within his competency. These meetings consider in a collegial manner new teachings and opinions, in whatever form they are disseminated, whose spread could be detrimental to faith and morals, apart from questions where, because the persons or the importance of the matter call for it, a request is made for a confidential meeting or a very special consultation. The ordinary session also resolves questions or doubts submitted by the *Congresso*, such as the possibility of a new examination of a question to be carried out by others; encourages research undertaken to deepen an understanding of the faith; proposes to the Pope the granting of graces (for example, dispensations); and judges the legal and factual issues regarding the *privilegium Fidei* and *graviora delicta*.

The plenary Session is convened ordinarily every two years to deal with matters of great importance and other specific questions of the Congregation as determined by Cardinal Prefect. All Cardinal and Bishop members take part, together with the Secretary of the Congregation; the Undersecretary and Promotor of Justice take part in matters within their competence, but do not vote.

Given the particular delicacy of matters treated by the Congregation of the Doctrine of the Faith, the greater part of its business is subject to the Pontifical Secret. This was established to replace the former Secret of the Holy Office and is a kind of secrecy confirmed by oath to protect cases and important decisions that concern the life of the Church, as well as to protect those persons who are bound to observe it. Already established by a special instruction from the Secretariat of State on 24 June 1968, this secret was once again required by a later *Instructio* from the same Secretariat of State and approved *ex audientia* by Paul VI on 4 February 1974. Sanctions for violating this oath are described in the *Regolamento generale della Curia Romana* (Articles 36 §2; 76 §1, 3°).

Decisions issued by the Congregation of the Doctrine of the Faith are doctrinal or disciplinary, depending on the nature of the case; and, because of their great importance, in some cases they must be approved by the Pope. Doctrinal documents, always approved by the Holy Father, participate therefore in the ordinary magisterium of the Supreme Pontiff. Documents published since the Second Vatican Council, which offer authoritative responses to new questions in such areas as Christology, ecclesiology, anthropology, liberation theology, the vocation of the theologian, and doctrine regarding the sacraments and morality, have been collected in the volume *Documenta inde a Concilio Vaticano secundo expleto edita* (1966-2005), Vatican City: Libreria Editrice Vaticana, 2005. These documents are available in English on the Vatican website: http.//www.vatican.va/roman_curia/congregations/cfaith. The electronic domain is: www.doctrinafidei.va

Doctrinal Examination

The procedure ordinarily followed for the doctrinal examination of books, other published materials, and any other communications that touch on matters of faith was set down in the special *Regolamento* of 1971, and further developed in the *Agendi ratio in doctrinarum examine* of

29 June 1997, according to which individual texts are examined that have been brought to the attention of the Congregation of the Doctrine of the Faith. This examination can be carried out either through an ordinary process or an urgent process, depending on the nature of the case.

The ordinary process is followed when a text – after a preliminary review by the Office, in which the original, authentic text is studied by the *Congresso* of the Congregation, assisted by consultors and experts – is thought to contain serious doctrinal errors, the identification of which calls for attentive discernment, but whose possible negative effect on the faithful does not seem to be particularly urgent.

The internal phase starts with the prior investigation, undertaken in the offices of the Congregation, beginning with the appointment of two or more experts who have the competence to examine the writing, express their opinion on its merits, and determine if the text "conforms to the doctrine of the Church" (Article 9). At the same time a relator is appointed on the author's behalf who has the specific task of showing in a spirit of truth the positive aspects of his teaching and the merits of the author, of cooperating in the authentic interpretation of his thought within its overall theological context, and of expressing a judgment regarding the influence of the author's opinions (Article 10). This is followed by a discussion in the *Consulta* in which not only the consultors take part, but the relator who speaks on behalf of the author, the author's Ordinary (who cannot be represented by another), and the experts who have prepared their opinions, in order to formulate a thorough evaluation of the text under consideration. At the end of this discussion, the consultors alone vote on the outcome of the examination and leave it to the Ordinary Session of the Congregation to determine "whether to present objections to the author, and if so, on which points" (Article 14). The decisions of the Ordinary Session are submitted to the Pope for approval.

If the internal process determines to proceed to a presentation of objections, the external phase begins. The Ordinary or Ordinaries concerned and the appropriate offices of the Roman Curia are informed. The list of erroneous or dangerous propositions at issue, together with explanatory argumentation and documentation, are communicated to the author and his advisor, whom the author has the right to nominate to assist him (Article 17). The author must present a written response within three months, which the *Congresso* examines to evaluate the arguments presented. If this examination reveals truly new doctrinal elements requiring further evaluation, it is then decided whether the question should again be presented to the *Consulta* and to the Ordinary Session, whose final decision must receive approval by the Pope before being communicated to the author's Ordinary, the Episcopal Conference, and the appropriate offices of the Roman Curia. Should the author not send the written response the Ordinary Session of the Congregation takes the appropriate decisions (Article 19).

In accord with Article 23 of the *Agendi ratio,* an urgent examination is employed "when the writing is clearly and certainly erroneous and, at the same time, its dissemination could cause or already has caused grave harm to the faithful." The speed with which the process takes place depends upon the gravity of the case under examination when it already represents a danger to the faithful. In this case, the Ordinary and concerned offices of the Curia are immediately informed of the process, and a Commission is appointed by the Congregation which is especially entrusted with "promptly determining the erroneous or dangerous propositions" (Article 24). The propositions identified by the Commission, together with the relative documentation, are submitted to the Ordinary Session. If the Commission judges that the propositions are in fact erroneous and dangerous, after the approval of the Holy Father, "they are transmitted to the author, through his Ordinary, with the request that they be corrected within two months."

In contrast to earlier norms, the present procedure has the merit of providing certain safeguards – the involvement of a relator acting on the author's behalf, the assistance of an advisor [*consigliere di fiducia*] if need be, the possibility of a personal meeting between the author and some representatives of the Congregation, and the participation of the author's Ordinary – to facilitate a resolution of the case.

LEGISLATION CONCERNING RESERVED DELICTS

In the treating of reserved delicts, the Congregation proceeds according to what is established in Saint John Paul II's motu proprio *Sacramentorum sanctitatis tutela*. This legislation contains precise substantive and procedural regulations. In 2010, Pope Benedict XVI revised the above-mentioned motu proprio in order to improve practical operations and to boost the effectiveness of the action of the Church. To guarantee a more rapid examination concerning the delicts reserved to the competence of the Congregation for the Doctrine of the Faith, with his rescript of 3 November 2014, Pope Francis instituted a special College, which the ordinary session of the Congregation has adopted for greater efficiency.

THE PONTIFICAL BIBLICAL COMMISSION

The Pontifical Biblical Commission was established by Leo XIII with the Apostolic Letter *Vigilantiae studiique memores* of 30 October 1902 with the specific purpose of resolving questions that might arise concerning the exact interpretation of Sacred Scripture and promoting progress in biblical studies. Soon after, Pius X broadened its purpose: it was allowed to confer academic degrees in biblical studies (the license and the doctorate); the manner of doing this was determined soon after with the Apostolic Letter *Scripturae sanctae* of 23 February 1904. Pius XI, with the motu proprio *Bibliorum scientia* of 27 April 1924 and the subsequent Constitution *Deus scientiarum Dominus* of 24 May 1931 made the degrees granted by the Commission equivalent to those awarded by pontifical universities.

Completely reformed by Paul VI with the motu proprio *Sedula cura* of 27 June 1971, the Pontifical Biblical Commission, although its proper structure remains unaltered, is now associated with the Congregation for the Doctrine of the Faith, whose Prefect serves as its President. It is composed of a Secretary (who is also a Consultor of the Congregation), an assistant Secretary, and twenty members chosen from among the most renowned biblical scholars. Non-Catholic biblical scholars can also be invited to work with its sub-commissions, although they are not members of the Commission. The responses given by the Commission are very important; they can be found on the Vatican website (with the more recent ones also translated into English) at: (http://www.vatican.va/roman_curia/congregation/cfaith). The most recent publications of the Commission have dealt with the following topics: *The Interpretation of the Bible in the Church* (1993); *The Jewish People and their Scriptures in the Christian Bible* (2001); and *The Bible and Morality: Biblical Roots of Christian Morality* (2008); *The Inspiration and Truth of Sacred Scripture.*

The Word that Comes from God and Speaks of God for the Salvation of the World (2014).

THE INTERNATIONAL THEOLOGICAL COMMISSION

The International Theological Commission was established by Paul VI on 11 April 1969, in response to a proposal made by the first Synod of Bishops, which met in October 1967. Its purpose is to assist the Holy See, and especially to work with the Congregation for the Doctrine of the Faith, in examining doctrinal questions of great importance. Presided over by the Prefect of the Congregation, it is made up of thirty members who are "devoted to the study of theological doctrine and faithful to the authentic doctrine of the teaching Church", as Paul VI declared in the consistory of 28 April 1969. Chosen from the most renowned theologians who are faithful to the Magisterium of the Church and representative of various schools and nations, all the members of the Commission are proposed by the Prefect (after consultation with the appropriate Episcopal Conferences) and appointed by the Pope and serve for five years.

This Commission, whose statutes were definitively approved by John Paul II with the motu proprio *Tredecim anni iam* of 6 August 1982, is required to hold a plenary assembly at least once a year, but it also carries out its activity by means of sub-commissions that are entrusted with the study of particular issues; these meet more frequently. The results of the studies undertaken by the International Theological Commission are first submitted to the Pope and then consigned to the Congregation so that they can be utilized in the most appropriate way. The documents published by the Commission have been collected, in Italian, in the volume *Commissione Teologica Internazionale. Documenta 1969-2004* (Bologna, Edizioni Studio Domenicano, 2004) and are available in English on the Vatican website: (http://www. vatican.va/roman_curia/congregation/cfaith). Some of the most important recent documents are: *The Interpretation of Dogma* (1990); *Some Current Questions in Eschatology* (1992); *Christianity and the World Religions* (1997); *Memory and Reconciliation: The Church and the Faults of the Past* (2000); *From the Diakonia of Christ to the Diakonia of the Apostles* (2003); *Communion and Stewardship: Human Persons Created in the Image of God* (2004); *The Hope of Salvation for Infants Who Die without Being Baptised* (2007); *In Search of Universal Ethic: A New Look at the Natural Law* (2009); *Theology Today: Perspectives, Principles and Criteria* (2012); and *God the Trinity and the Unity of Humanity. Christian Monotheism and its Opposition to Violence* (2014).

THE PONTIFICAL COMMISSION *ECCLESIA DEI*

The Pontifical Commission *Ecclesia Dei* was established by John Paul II with the motu proprio *Ecclesia Dei* of 2 July 1988 with the "task of collaborating with the bishops, with the Departments of the Roman Curia and with the circles concerned, for the purpose of facilitating full ecclesial communion of priests, seminarians, religious communities or individuals until now linked in various ways to the Fraternity founded by Archbishop Lefebvre, who may wish to remain united to the Successor Peter in the Catholic Church". The Commission exercises the authority of the Holy See over institutions and religious communities established by it, which have as their proper rite the Extraordinary Form of the Roman Rite. The Commission has responsibility for providing pastoral care to the faithful throughout the world who observe the earlier Latin liturgical traditions.

With the motu proprio *Summorum pontificum* of 7 July 2007 Benedict XVI broadened the authority of the Commission, and with the motu proprio *Ecclesiae unitatem* of 2 July 2009 he updated its structure, connecting it firmly to the Congregation for the Doctrine of the Faith.

The Commission is presided over by the Prefect of the Congregation for the Doctrine of the Faith, and is made up of a Secretary and several officials. The Commission's responsibility includes dealing with major questions regarding the celebration of the Mass and sacraments in the Extraordinary Form, and integrating groups associated with earlier liturgical forms into full communion with the Church. Questions of a doctrinal nature are submitted ordinarily to the Congregation for the Doctrine of the Faith and then submitted to the Supreme Pontiff for approval.

DOCUMENTATION

APPENDIX 1

List of Cardinal Secretaries (1602-1966) and Prefects (since 1966)

CAMILLO BORGHESE (Paul V): 1602 – 16 May 1605

POMPEO ARRIGONE: 1605 – 4 April 1616

GIOVANNI GARSIA MILLINI: 1616 – 2 October 1629

ANTONIO BARBERINI: 1629-1633

FRANCESCO BARBERINI: 1633-1679

CESARE FACCHINETTI: 1679-1683

ALDERANO CIBO: 1683-1700

GALEAZZO MARESCOTTI: 1700-1716

FABRIZIO SPADA: 1716 – 15 June 1717

NICCOLÒ ACCIAIOLI: 1717 – 23 February 1719

FRANCESCO GIUDICE: 1719 – 10 October 1725

FABRIZIO PAOLUCCI: 1725 – 12 June 1726

PIETRO OTTOBONI: 14 June 1726 – 28 February 1740

TOMMASO RUFFO: 29 August 1740 – 16 February 1753

NERI MARIA CORSINI: 26 February 1753 – 6 December 1770

GIOVANNI FRANCESCO STOPPANI: 12 December 1770 – 18 November 1774

LUIGI MARIA TORRIGIANI: 22 February 1775 – 6 January 1777

CARLO REZZONICO: 17 January 1777 – 26 January 1799

LEONARDO ANTONELLI: 8 November 1800 – 23 January 1811

GIULIO MARIA DELLA SOMAGLIA: 1814 – 30 March 1830

BARTOLOMEO PACCA: 5 April 1830 – 19 April 1844

VINCENZO MACCHI: 25 April 1844 – 30 September 1860

COSTANTINO PATRIZI: 3 October 1860 – 17 December 1876

PROSPERO CATERINI: 21 December 1876 – 28 October 1881

ANTONIO MARIA PANEBIANCO: 30 March 1882 – 25 January 1883

LUIGI BILIO: 25 January 1883 – 30 January 1884

RAFFAELE MONACO LA VALLETTA: 15 February 1884 – 14 July 1896

LUCIDO MARIA PAROCCHI: 5 August 1896 – 15 January 1903

SERAFINO VANNUTELLI: 17 January 1903 – 31 December 1908

MARIANO RAMPOLLA DEL TINDARO: 31 December 1908 – 16 December 1913

DOMENICO FERRATA: 2 January – 10 October 1914

RAFFAELE MERRY DEL VAL: 14 October 1914 – 26 February 1930

DONATO SBARRETTI: 4 July 1930 – 1 April 1939

FRANCESCO MARCHETTI SELVAGGIANI: 30 April 1939 – 13 January 1951

GIUSEPPE PIZZARDO: 15 February 1951 – 7 November 1959

ALFREDO OTTAVIANI: 12 January – 7 November 1959 (Pro-Secretary); 7 November 1959 – 9 February 1966 (Secretary); 9 February 1966 – 6 January 1968 (Pro-Prefect)

FRANJO ŠEPER: 8 January 1968 – 25 November 1981 (Prefect)

JOSEPH RATZINGER (BENEDICT XVI): 25 November 1981 – 2 April 2005

WILLIAM JOSEPH LEVADA: 13 May 2005 – 2 July 2012

GERHARD LUDWIG MÜLLER: since 2 July 2012

APPENDIX 2

Apostolic letter
given motuproprio
Integrae servandae
Pope Paul VI

Roman Pontiffs, in union with the college of
Bishops, have over the course of centuries and
amidst human vicissitudes guarded the deposit of
revealed Religion, entrusted to them by God to
be preserved integrally, so that up to this day they
have transmitted it intact, not without the inter-
vention of Divine help, for through them the Holy
Spirit acts, who is as the soul of the Mystical Body
of Christ.

However, the Church, which is of divine institution and deals with divine matters, is made up
of men and lives among people: thus, in order to
fulfill her duties, she employs different instruments
according to the various times and human cultures,
having to treat numerous and important matters,
because the Roman Pontiffs themselves and the
Bishops, concerned innumerable matters, would
not be able to provide for them alone. It is therefore from the very nature of things that administra-
trative organs have come into being, i.e. the Curia:
to them was entrusted the task of facilitating the
government of the Church by supervising the observance of laws promulgated, by promoting initia-

tives in order to realize the Church's proper finality, and by resolving any controversies that might arise.

It is no wonder then, if, with time's changing conditions, modifications are introduced in such organisms: and in reality more than once in the past Roman Pontiffs, Our Predecessors, have taken pains to introduce reforms into the structure of the Roman Curia; in this respect those especially worth mentioning are the Constitutions *Immensa Aeterni Dei* of Sixtus V and *Sapienti Consilio* of Pius X, the provisions of which have been almost entirely incorporated into the Code of Canon Law.

However, after these Constitutions, even after the promulgation of the said Code, situations and times have changed greatly, just as We ourselves pronounced during a Discourse to the Cardinals and staff of the Roman Curia on 21 September 1963 (cf. *AAS* 55 (1963), p. 793ss.).

These things having been considered and the advice of Our Venerable Brother Cardinals and of Bishops having been sought, We have decreed that a certain reform of the Roman Curia be realized. And there is no doubt that the reform should begin with the Sacred Congregation of the Holy Office, for the reason that to this Congregation the most important matters of the Roman Curia are entrusted, as in truth are the doctrine concerning faith and morals and the causes most strictly related to such doctrine.

On 21 July 1542 Our Beloved Predecessor Paul III, with the Apostolic Constitution *Licet ab initio* founded the Supreme Sacred Congregation of the Universal Roman Inquisition to which he entrusted as its proper end the duty of persecuting heresy and consequently of suppressing crimes against the faith, of prohibiting dangerous books and of appointing Inquisitors for the whole Church. Very often its power was extended to other matters, either because of their difficult nature or because of their singular importance.

In 1908, as the name Universal Roman Inquisition was not best suited to the conditions of the time, Saint Pius X with the Constitution *Sapienti Consilio* changed it to the "Congregation of the Holy Office".

But, because there is *no fear* in love (1 Jn 4:18), the defense of the faith is now better served by promoting doctrine, in such a way that, while errors stand corrected and those who err are gently called back to the truth, heralds of the Gospel may find new strength. Moreover, the advance of human culture, whose the importance the religious field must not overlook, is that the faithful follow the directives of the Church with greater adhesion and love, if, insofar as in matters of faith and morals it is possible to make clear to them the reasons for definitions and laws.

So, that from now on this Sacred Congregation may more perfectly fulfill its role in promoting the sound doctrine and efficacy of the Church in the most important works of apostolate, in virtue of Our Supreme Apostolic Authority we have established the following norms to alter its name and its regulation:

1. That which was hitherto called the *Sacred Congregation of the Holy Office* will become the *Congregation for the Doctrine of the Faith*, whose duty it is

to safeguard doctrine on faith and morals in the whole Catholic world.

2. It is presided over by the Supreme Pontiff and directed by the Cardinal Secretary with the help of an Assessor, of a Substitute and of the Promotor of Justice.

3. All questions which regard the doctrine on faith and morals or which touch upon the faith are within the competence of the Congregation.

4. It examines new teachings and new opinions in whatever way they are spread, it promotes studies in this area, and encourages the Congresses of scholars; it condemns those teachings found to be contrary to the principles of the faith, after, however, having heard the view of the Bishops of those regions, if they are specifically connected with the issues.

5. It carefully examines books that have been reported and, if necessary, condemns them, after, however, having heard the author, to whom is given the faculty to defend himself, also in writing, and not without having notified the Ordinary, as was already established in the Constitution *Sollicita ac Provida* by Our Predecessor of happy memory Benedict XIV.

6. Likewise it is its duty to deal legally or in fact with questions regarding the privilege of faith.

7. It is also its duty to judge delicts crimes against the faith, according to the norms of ordinary procedure.

8. It provides for the protection of the dignity of the Sacrament of Penance, by proceeding according to the amended and approved norms that will be communicated to the Ordinaries, giving the

sinner the faculty to defend himself or to choose a defender from among those authorized by the Congregation.

9. It maintains appropriate relations with the Pontifical Commission for Biblical Studies.

10. The Congregation employs a group of Consultors whom the Supreme Pontiff appoints from men around the world who are distinguished for their doctrine, prudence and expertise. If the matter to be dealt with so requires, the Consultors can be added to the experts, chosen particularly from University professors.

11. The Congregation proceeds in two ways: either administrative or judicial, according to the diverse nature of the matters to be dealt with.

12. The internal regulation of the Congregation will be made public through a particular Instruction.

What has been decreed by us in this Letter *Motu Proprio data*, we command be observed and ratified notwithstanding anything to the contrary.

Given in Rome, at St Peter's, 7 December 1965, the third year of Our Pontificate.

PAULUS PP. VI

APPENDIX 3

Apostolic Constitution
Pastor bonus (Articles 48-55) of John Paul II

ART. 48

The proper duty of the Congregation for the Doctrine of the Faith is to promote and safeguard the doctrine on faith and morals in the whole Catholic world; so it has competence in things that touch this matter in any way.

ART. 49

Fulfilling its duty of promoting doctrine, the Congregation fosters studies so that the understanding of the faith may grow and a response in the light of the faith may be given to new questions arising from the progress of the sciences or human culture.

ART. 50

It helps the bishops, individually or in groups, in carrying out their office as authentic teachers and doctors of the faith, an office that carries with it the duty of promoting and guarding the integrity of that faith.

ART. 51

To safeguard the truth of faith and the integrity of morals, the Congregation takes care lest faith or morals suffer harm through errors that have been spread in any way whatever. Wherefore:

1. it has the duty of requiring that books and other writings touching faith or morals, being published by the Christian faithful, be subjected to prior examination by the competent authority;

2. it examines carefully writings and opinions that seem to be contrary or dangerous to true faith, and, if it is established that they are opposed to the teaching of the Church, reproves them in due time, having given authors full opportunity to explain their minds, and having forewarned the Ordinary concerned; it brings suitable remedies to bear, if this be opportune.

3. finally, it takes good care lest errors or dangerous doctrines, which may have been spread among the Christian people, do not go without apt rebuttal.

Art. 52

The Congregation examines offences against the faith and more serious ones both in behaviour or in the celebration of the sacraments which have been reported to it and, if need be, proceeds to the declaration or imposition of canonical sanctions in accordance with the norms of common or proper law.

Art. 53

It is to examine whatever concerns the privilege of the faith, both in law and in fact.

Art. 54

Documents being published by other dicasteries of the Roman Curia, insofar as they touch on the doctrine of faith or morals, are to be subjected to its prior judgement.

Art. 55

Established within the Congregation for the Doctrine of the Faith are the Pontifical Biblical Commission and the International Theological Commission, which act according to their own approved norms and are presided over by the cardinal prefect of this Congregation.

INDEX

VATICAN PRESS